Lisa Robertson

XEclogue

GRAPHICS BY KELLY WOOD

New Star Books
Vancouver
2012

NEW STAR BOOKS LTD.
#107 – 3477 Commercial Street
Vancouver, BC V5N 4E8 CANADA

1574 Gulf Road, #1517
Point Roberts, WA 98281 USA

www.NewStarBooks.com info@NewStarBooks.com

Designed and typeset at The Cardigan Press
Originally published 1993 by Tsunami Editions
Revised edition published 1999 by New Star Books
Reprinted 2006, 2012

LIBRARY AND ARCHIVES CANADA
CATALOGUING IN PUBLICATION

Robertson, Lisa
XEclogue

Poems.
ISBN 0-921586-72-8
I. Wood, Kelly, 1962– II. Title.
PS8585.03217X42 1999 C811'.54 C99-910977-4
PR9199.3.R5316X42 1999

Printed in Canada by Imprimerie Gauvin

MIX
Paper from responsible sources
FSC® C100212

X Eclogue

For my Grandmothers

Nature is not natural and that is natural enough.

– Gertrude Stein

XEclogue

How Pastoral A PROLOGUE

I NEEDED A GENRE for the times that I go phantom. I needed a genre to rampage Liberty, haunt the foul freedom of silence. I needed to pry loose Liberty from an impacted marriage with the soil. I needed a genre to gloss my ancestress' complicity with a socially expedient code; to invade my own illusions of historical innocence. The proud trees, the proud rocks, the proud sky, the proud fields, the proud poor have been held before my glazed face for centuries. I believed they were reflections. The trees leaned masochistically into my absence of satisfaction. The horizon pulled me close. It was trying to fulfil a space I thought of as my body. Through the bosco a fleecy blackness revealed the nation as its vapid twin. Yet nostalgia can locate those structured faults our embraces also seek. A surface parts. The nasty hours brim with the refinements of felicity. It's obvious now: Liberty has been dressed in the guise of an ambivalent expenditure.

My ancestress would not wait for me. I began to track her among the elegant tissue of echoes, quotations, shadows on the deepening green. Because she bore no verifiable identity, I decided to construct her from kisses: puckers and fissures in use, and also from the flaking traces of her brittle skirt. For I needed someone not useful to me, but obnoxious, prosthetic, and irrelevant as my gender. Let's say Nature, like femininity, is obsolete. She's simply a phantom who indolently twists the melancholic mirror of sex. Far into the rural distance, the horizon splays beneath her florid grip. In deep sleep, my ancestress tells me a story:

"Ontology is the luxury of the landed. Let's pretend you 'had' a land. Then you 'lost' it. Now fondly describe it. That is pastoral. Consider your homeland, like all utopias, obsolete. Your pining rhetoric points to obsolescence. The garden gate shuts firmly. Yet Liberty must remain throned in her posh gazebo. What can the poor Lady do? Beauty, Pride, Envy, the Bounteous Land, the Romance of Citizenship: these mawkish paradigms flesh out the nation, fard its empty gaze. What if, for your new suit, you chose to parade obsolescence? Make a parallel nation, an anagram of the Land. Annex Liberty, absorb her, and recode her: infuse her with your nasty optics. The anagram will surpass and delete the first world, yet, in all its elements, remain identical. Who can afford sincerity? It's an expensive monocle."

When I awake I find myself in a new world. The buildings, the clothes, the trees are no more or less coy than they were, yet I had been so intent on the dense, lush words that I had not realized a world could be subtracted from her fruiting skin. The old locutions could only lose themselves in that longed-for landscape; but now I pluck for myself "peace in our own time" and the desuetude of nostalgia. It's as if suddenly a pitcher of slim flowers needled that monumental absence of regret. So elegant, so precise, so evil, all the pleasures have become my own.

ECLOGUE ONE *Honour*

I HAVE FELT REGRET but turn now to the immensity of a rhythm that in the midst of her own mettle was invisible. I'll describe the latinate happiness that appears to me as small tufted syllables in the half-light, greenish and quivering as grasses. Ah, the tidy press of the catalogue, the knotted plantlets of a foiled age, the looming test of our grim diaphany, let me embrace these as the lost term "honour" while I lace this high pink boot I call Felicity.

(Lady M finds her thoughts a little agitated; her sight wanders and is fed by an artificial rudeness whose particular odour floods her mind. It's as if she were dreaming on a bus.)

Watered patterns sway lit beneath the air or beneath the movement of air. Fine grey pigments cling so pungently with such rich spread that it's all dainty and silken as the fickle-stench of the sibilant and caressed name "Nancy." The teen-aged multitude drifts off to a grainy and torpid horizon; they stroke the crude till it compels or decadently blooms. Banality stokes their punctual lust for the familiar; branches, courage, obligation stalk as cathartic yellow splays among roots. Weeds often seem sardonic as the measured tactics of a cold strut; yet if leisure were conquered this landscape would gauntly bud and split into the cold texture embroidered on the lurid skin of a leaf.

Or: careful field quincuncial as the exhaustive and private happiness spilt from a necklace of januaries. Knots, compartments and grottos cannot compare to a field's livid frisk, neither to the ridgie factions near the pompous arch. Yet the sky's tolerably liberal and apt to supplement a bitchy little tapestry, in the way the light in a painting seems fringed or redolent as a pimp, in the way a teenager will flagrantly caress a name with paint. Read this orchard as the Roaring Boys who course the town at night: tawdry, flecked and billowing behind their silky fluted pricks, their short lines syncopate as ripe fruits shake the lawn.

Or: she's in the landscape without ambiguity and it's to a trim cloister she lends her tendentious support. Wind preens or lustres the elegant weeds; obligation splices cold and keeps darkening and brooding. The weedy ruffling of Nancy's sheathed hips absorbs a thought quicker than the lagging wind. Everything patterns a differing lag – the flanked and massy sky turns decorative as it clusters or nearly punctuates her torpor. The Roaring Boys fan back; they coil poignantly beneath the moral clusters of their blue groves. The roaring angels are alert as nets and their sly pricks nudge the cold.

LADY M *I feel hapless when I think of the buttery and peculiar flowers we dub the monikers of our malaise.*

NANCY *Yet it's so plucky and slightly ruffled . . .*

LADY M *As this dim foliage we stride through. Nancy, what of "paradise" or "harmony"? It's so leather-like in unreality –*

NANCY *We're professionals. I see your face in the rain.*

LADY M *Like a grim violet.*

NANCY *I push you away*
I fall to the floor
It's a mixed-up world
With shook-up love.

LADY M *My back's to the wall. How can such slim felicity so bruise the trees?*

NANCY *You call this filial conduct? Stop there. I hear the Boys:*

ROARING BOYS (*singing*):

Hey Blushing Berries, you've got us curious. Groves
Nodding can't masque your emotion's curious
Fretwork. We need consolement. We're no strangers
To the quick whirls of russet-wrapt or bluish
Emotion, pendant, typical, sultry, fringed
Like a bump on the horizon. Our reddened silks
Rustle with profession. Imitation cramps
Such rudeness: But those games just aren't interesting.
Take this hint – we're typical Boys, our fickle emotion
Wanders and is fed, yet we choose
To dedicate our follies to you. Shall we syncopate
The several beauties known by the name of the Purling
Stream? This tumult's meant to tilt
All grammar. We're just those that
Want you to feel . . .

Dear Nancy,

Quietly, evil as a concept's disappeared and I'm not sorry to judge the smoothed-over garden dangerous. I've indulged my curiosity in all the horrid graces, thought swelling or swollen, conscious anyway that the motive seemed creepy – but it seemed natural. Their diction's pleasure unwound me, though I knew it doggerel, and they mere poetasters. They've not advanced from the flimsy past: it's just the tumult of a pendant usage, it's just the sultry horror of that fake forest. Choric swains that call me Berry miss the point – dirty little swains playing at the mouth of the gemmy cave, fraying my nerves with their meticulous blossoms. So I'll loosen up to describe their limbs as botanical manifestations of small irksome enjambments, styleless as numbered doors. Yet silk and cotton and solid some bird or some robin flew through the somewhat florid expansion once named as my heart. It was noonish and the pinch held out to a person anyone would name trouble . . . a girl whose instinct for trend was marginalized and pointless. But I wanted something new, something way past the florid radicalism of the Marxist cashbar. I wanted the stuff that joyriders run on: that queer touched-up light that transmits over the air; miming a tension, living on the crux of a regime which could slide to the coy illusion of Liberty.

Typical girls – whose liberty leaches and fans from a porous border, who fold like fans, who trick the eating class – typical girls explain to me the use of the word "Liberty." I'd fall to the floor for their smooth gesture, their opaque and viscous oil-like drag, their porous border, their controlled iridescence, their drag and tooth, the gnarled yet polished scent of evil. When I'm trying to think about the word "russet" I use fan-like tactics borrowed from the girls, though vagueness signals, almost breaks my purple spite. It's not easy to define my feeling of a reddened peace of mind, a ruffled, shattered, mixed-up world. How can silence or expression stop? All these sluttish thickets and rivulets of green, all these bitchy, sybaritic flickers of leaf only simulate my technical and carminine thirst for the smooth sensation of felicity. A spilt necklace makes a curious fretwork; yet I've indulged my curiosity within a knot, judging the drag and density viscous and gaunt. Maybe it wasn't the girl, maybe the Boys took a smile from their package – it was raining, they weren't looking at me – maybe they've wreathed their instinct for thought.

There's no need for crying. Honour nor emotion's not so squalid and swindled as all that, though I feel the grim vibrations of the darkening air, I feel the horrid crackling transmit through my skin and hair. It's so reptilian like those weird things that scuttle underfoot, lend their frenzied rhythm to my thought
those peculiar monikers
those russet quivering stalks
those lags
those plantlets
those elegant and massy coils
Nancy, how can these be *Thought*?

– Lady M

ECLOGUE TWO *Beauty*

WHEN I WAS LOUNGING in the Grove I saw a Vision: it was like a flickering screen reporting a very pleasant history of love, thick-set with trees and starred with flowers and diverse fountains, all belonging to the sweet or to the dangerous affairs of love. I interpreted the image then drew up these two books as my oblation.

I

A bolder strapping girl would kiss
To dress and trim would be her entertainment
For time is thick, opalesque, and shady and watered
And yesterday a boy appeared with apples in his hand
With wanton romping and hoitie-toitie he kept
A cunning thing that would not be caught
He flung the berries at her and pulled the finest flowers
And what is Love? Is he a boy or a bird?
And sprung to a grove, skipt to the top
Then she saw his wings and little dart
And knew all flowers are his work.

I have known a bull to run bellowing as if prickt with a goad
And I myself, when I was young, forgot to eat
Tedious nights never could compose my panting
As if thwackt and bashed back and sides
Yet could not draw the froward girl
She's small and slim and so will slip away
We've clipt and kissed and that's as good as nothing.
What rare harnesses and ornaments – all are lost on her face.

Then fell into deep sleep, and those three appeared
Big women, gorgeous and teased
And in all things like their statues.
The eldest spoke:

> *Girl that stands under pine, honoured with flowers*
> *Get up and stop fretting*
> *For she shall come certainly tomorrow*
> *Or I am quite broke and must give up my trade.*

Then the second:

> *We took pity on you and gave you the orchard.*

The youngest then uttered:

> *Start up out of sleep, take your pleasure and grief*
> *And adore us: Give us the best.*

I took up the pipes and boughs to make them happy
And the Boys howled like dogs in the woods:

Crass love fucks under shade trees
Explicit cries burst under little whips of vine
The grass itself a ferociously docile chorus
Cruiser! Your little urge is divinely thrown!

This gem's purple tint annuls flowers
Palpitates under a frond's breath
Urgent, not tentative, the roving light Night only can relinquish
Sparks shy liquids.

Gutters tumble, the green-rimmed spring imbibes us;
I'm minus merit under the flux of this girl's
Pure bridge. Why nurse regret?
The stirred earth kneels for her fat moans.

If a pretty sip would cruise Love's shy tremour
If gems like flames decked her purple lisp
I'd merit a nod more than pudor suggests
Crushed rubies which lately ignite my rest.

This new diva lets the girls use her couch
To ply their lilies – Yet you protest?
Love will feast, so wisdom's vexed
They're nimble, flash a fierce aroma.

She's very roguish; your pudor reflects it
She wills you to venture indiscreetly for a girl
For three nights the kids have partied
Clustered in the park, drunk for her.

Flowers crush under us, we're teased and casual
Not sated yet, nor is poetry
Hesitant – the perverse night can't rest
You're bound in silver Nancy – now receive delight.

As if you were born to explain April to us;
A kiss that cuts can't wet or gild the leaves
Her long arms rest like fronds in the baleful green
That used song of yours won't touch the Lady's need.

She sits hybrid at the Dairy Queen
Among ripe prayers and lures – fanning Psyche's
Louche stuff – adores calendars. Hi Psyche!
That's some kit: schools quit for its languor.

I'm loquacious or raucous, swanning for the fun of it
But I'd sooner tear the subtle moss from under poplars
Than he should put a note of love into her golden mouth:
I'll nudge the queer sorrow her barbarity merits.

In her dream of Justice
Like a crease soaked in the purple spume of boys' tears
Or a black stem under a hoof
Undulant Diane drinks her straight.

II

What is this tint that in the shrill cress
Will never cease to trouble us and in the fields
Gives prick and praise for Beauty?
And said birds that feed on berries
Are pervious – and shook the snow from his thighs.
I thought of nothing carefully, but of snow, and the birds.
Then kissed the cup and sipped a little
Though almost choked drank slowly
Tickled with strange measure
She faked a pretty anger
I entertained the night with fantastic, empty pleasure
We went as far as the ivie-bush
And ivie-crowns upon our heads
And carried her kiss untouched and entire
Then all was fresh, inclined
To wriggle and nussle and lascivious
Ardent leaps. In the thickest of the wood
Bid him kiss close and often
And directed him to her fancie
The ground had a sweeter scent, the boughs a blush
One fruit, rare and rich, would outdo many together
She was wild to climb the tree
Nor would she be forbidden
She seized the apple and put it in her bosom.

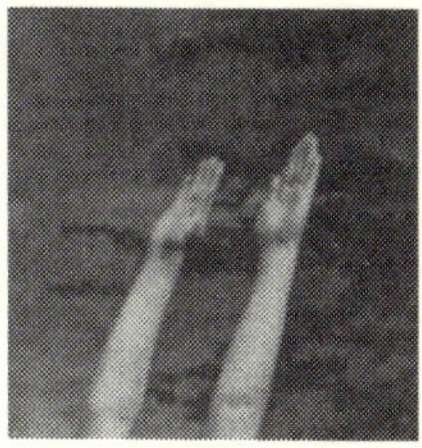

ECLOGUE THREE *Liberty*

WHAT FOLLOWS IS the interminable journal of culture. This neutral and emotive little word seems, in the operatic dark green woods, so harmless and legal but it's liberty totalized, an incommensurable crime against the girls. To question privilege I'm going to shame this word. I will begin by gathering around my body all the facts, for they affect my person. Consider my feeling of resentment. I could have used it to fortify my courage. But everything was happening very fast and I thought it would be a waste to use it then. Violence and deceit, contempt and envy changed their colour, enclosed our labour. The phantom body now buttresses the vilest swindles with sub-Garbo hauteur. Violence and contempt, deceit and envy, sabotage my method and I learn to love it. I am aware that I bring horror – I embody the problem of the free-rider, inconveniencing the leaf-built, the simple-hearted, the phobic, with the unctuous display of my grief:

Enormous grief as if outside "our culture" a sense of peace floated or languished with no historical precedent. As if we could *invent* liberty, as if peace and liberty had no place in that slow starvation. As if, subject only to "the laws of nature," a gendered life were worth three years or nothing. As if, allowed to believe and to own and to publish, newly hurled from the impartial sun, a person's coy reticence meant fraternity. As if nervous yet flung yet decorative – someone a noun discarded – this sweetie went down on a khaki blanket glittering.

Superlative mistress who hurts! My grief is no accident. I am hovering between plunder and awe. I am howling though the thick accretions of liberty, not harmonious, not patterned, but inconceivably voluptuous as thick rope. The enchanted world of harmonies has disappeared! The martyred world has disappeared! And I am not sorry for I tingle with the exquisite cadence of boredom – that flower's prodigious purple! If you slowly gilded flowers (or didn't), fact: this slow bloom holds the buttery promise of a meaning.

I want to remember how, couched in a tone like a windy cotton sleeve, the parenthetical real girls shuck the empire of convenience. The aristocracy of irony has never been their riskiest hope. They loll in the incommensurability of embarrassment, the semi-honesty of their slick membranes. Felicity is their glamour, the key. I have chosen for my fate their verdant garment and also the particular verdures of Libertie. For the image does not need me: rather I feel it is my calling to annotate the sheathed cadence of life beside power. Yet I don't mean to seem fantastic in the old sense. When I say "life beside power" I mean destruct the formal destinies, destruct the phantom body, destruct defunct ritual, unlock that paradise I mentioned earlier and give them back a renovated flower. (For whose utopia, peopled with sorrow, will annul such mollifying tokens?) Before turning I need to repeat that pornographic verb "to mollify."

What is this thought that refuses to reverse itself, that in the cool shade of fantasy creates an institution? that, shot-silk at the turn of a fold, not constructed but pursued, satisfies my kilted wit? Beardless boys stripped to the waist might illustrate my ability to think, but, like any experts in hope, they'd just deflate my perfect barbarity. If you took this prudish ornament, exuding moody sex as his own ornament, with his woozy shimmer, his bobbing glamour, fondler of the long-sleeved and lobed, he'd poach. Which means I must invent my own. So, by stepping from that house, I celebrate the death of method: the flirting woods call it, the glittering rocks call it – utopia is dead. High Loveliness was born *here* to cut back prim sublimity. She's a member of the lily tribe whose materials follow themselves. She's a bitch of the inauthentic; her ego's in drag. I flaunt her on my pink finger flipping backwards for Libertie into the saline crux of a lily. She's lying in the pagan flowers, sweet-faced in her pompous velvet, swathed in the crude luxury of my rhetoric, strewn with the petals of aptly faded hope.

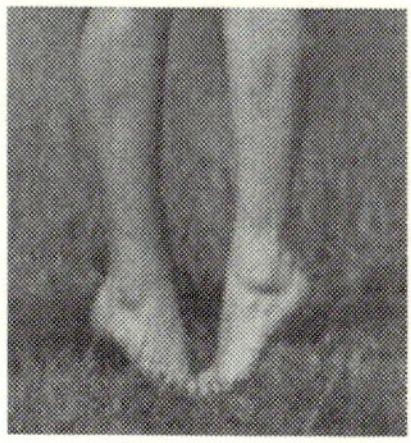

ECLOGUE FOUR *Cathexis*

All the flowers are glass flowers and looking into them the senses would vibrate in a gelatinous thrum. Each leaf's a sumptuous dervish; hurled from the vasty sun, its fretted points so hard and bright and tangy, it leaves a feeling of dangling – yet, with an oily ease, fronds like a fern's give hint to the deep blue minutes the green boys take. The hot dark stippled tints are indefatigably pleasurable and like widows or hairpins the mitten-shaped leaves are really those pleasures that do not, like those of the world, disappoint your expectations. All these briskly flecked notions sieve through a giddy tissue, unnatural red and rubbed grainless as if a green touch had deferred or shucked history.

(GOLDEN AND CRUEL, a lewdly nuanced ethic leaches from the girl with the abstract thighs. She's a connoisseur of pomposity: nor will pout nor yield a cadence outside the specific tenderness of the caked or couched. Horrible small symbolism is repressive and gives pleasure. Another evening pleats her nap so virtue's riddled or smacked; in a little while sensation will unlace.)

NANCY *I need to assume my dream of justice really does exist. Together shall we discover those conventions which, by giving or selling what has belonged to us, having known such green and felicitous hours, we renounce as we turn to the imagined lives of our polished rosewood dolls?*

A rosewood doll like an undulant carnivore who with voices of silk repeats the word leaf. Or walks the floor folding her fans, or, in a moment of alarm more intricate than the delicate rosewood spine, unlooses silk in salacious clots, blown flowers whose target dissipates or understands cloth – without aim – as libertines or cathrinettes or withered adjectives. Take for instance this Lola posed against the bustle with double hearts and sulky bits –

LADY M *I've walked through the gate and awoken – I feel my hands are incognito and fringed. I've seen all that can be called lovely. I fancy myself upon an idle fellow, boats passing and repassing with so slow a motion, all massy silver under the stiff wild vines – I roll the still boy out . . .*

I tumble in the luminous musculature
Of an ideology
Swift and pretty, enclosed as the edged-zest
Cross-sex jut of knowledge
As Romance is French, bombastic
End-stopped, supple, passing as a tulip-shaped
End-stopped panic epistemology, legitimate
Fantasy. Chthonic Machine! I'm compelled
To shun
The blue jut (gigantic gist)
"I'm torn between passion and honour."

NANCY *Consider the swell light of the social as floral, as reflexive, so compelled to shun sex or the museum. The task would be to reveal the metaphoric function of the gala lining of our favourite coat. Romance hedged; swift cathexis or villainess escapes actual repertoire of gender stuck to the heart like a spurious clone.*

LADY M *Don't look away! The quiet gets me. This little thicket is my portion, my supple jacket is lined with a humming. Here's what troubles me: erotic capital; families of women; utopic capital. When I describe shame as floral a weird little freedom is my equalizer. I'm all flattened out and swayless as if, secret and dark, birds flew in a grid at night. Erotic capital shifts, renovates the bosco. I feel as if there is so little time!*

ROARING BOYS (*singing*):

Come hither, Iron and Pearl, into the trees
Cleaner and more modern than
Worked fur when fur shows up a dark bruise
Or days filled with mud-resting demons
As brushed qualms
Slipping into waxed purses shaking like milk.

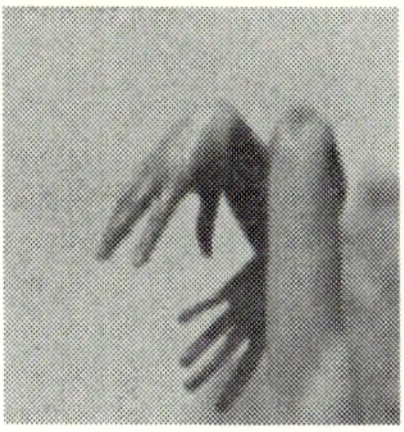

ECLOGUE FIVE *Phantasie*

. . . Four p.m.

I WANT TO TELL YOU about the hegemony of my supple extensions. My pliant starlets float like symptoms. They float in the indicative case, flinging accusations, insults, blasphemies and curses. They're cerebral and illegal. They force me to ask – by what aberration do I submit myself to some dead parody of growth, the rotting pastiche of the abject, a morbid inertia? Events congeal into image with no social aggression. The dream-truth is somewhere back in those fake ruins. Picture it snipped, mid-construction, ripped, recut, labiate, fitting so tightly your torso feels molded. Sound rushes ahead of the edge of the cut in big nasty syllables. My starlets don't need art and its cheating edifice. They're ham-fisted and redolent. They project their phantasie on my body:

We invented power. Power is a pink prosthesis hidden in the forest. Between black pines we strap it on and dip our pink prosthesis in the pool. The plastic glitters with clips and buckles beneath the surface of the pool. Breasts are a buttoned wedge held by buckled straps. Freedom is this extra size. We display it to the creaking forest. Also ride horses between our giant new limbs. Our pink bodies are giant and they own us for playing. The glittering giantesses are playing in the dark.

I'm thinking of this as a huge screen fluttering with smeared darks and obscene pastels, but I can feel it on my skin: the scratching seams of plastic, the coniferous movement of air, the lustrous flesh of animals.

Tenderheart, what should I say? We were not sleeping in the woods made of ravellings and worn flutings. Her hair was aubergine in the sodium light. Profuse and recurrent, so very mauve decade, we would "radiate" as if dressed only in our larded size. But I have been too literal. Never in rosedom would a seam, a cut, three shifters, and the hinged pink limbs of dolls replace that lost photograph: being in the dark forest and the deer glowing at the edge of it and the visual sense of quiet. I awake, "free-born, and about the age of thirty," to discover myself a traitoress.

ECLOGUE SIX *Nostalgia*

(THIS IS HOW Lady M enters: Sinuously flanked by Roaring Boys who pan her stance with flicks of birch; spouting the nonsense of swans; swagged in the mulberry light; on molten silks; flaunting the lovely ambiguity of the word "Grace.")

LADY M *Splendid ardour most obviously mine! April is a mere tuck in your shirt.*

NANCY *You're menacing and delirious. Your face could go back . . .*

LADY M *Which brings me irrevocably to the sulking plums: The dusk is a precise record . . .*

NANCY *Of the deadly metonymy of your hips.*

LADY M *I was raised a girl. I found myself my best possession.*

NANCY *Or looser hip whose elegance ribbons my yard.*

LADY M *I choose my fate.*

NANCY *Like those whose phantasies condemn us.*

The woods are retrospective; they shelter biographies, histories and criticisms. Why should not Lady M also enjoy their glooms and solitudes as analysts? Through the hedged wilds, the evening is coming, indefatigable as memory, then falling. So tarnished and so languid, it leaks the jargon of the barbarously pedantic. Lady M, among the glowing birch, thinks of the tapered, the flexible, the curious; differently, in succession, together. She is emptied by the clear bent of that succulent question which seems to pose itself regardless of the light.

Dear Nancy,

It's the same day. I had meant to read you the word in my purse – a word like lipstick, petulant and sentimental as a dress, yet complicit with your smudged revolution. But I let the moment pass, and now I must risk censure and speak of my shimmering girlhood – for the politics of girls cannot refuse nostalgia.

To be raised as a girl was a language, a system of dreaming fake dreams. In the prickling grass in the afternoon in August, I kept trying to find a place where my blood could rush. That was the obsolete expedience of hope. But yield to the evidence. And do not decline to interpret. A smooth span of nostalgia dissects the crackling gazebo. I close my eyes.

A girl named Queen Beauty is in the midst of horses. She's born in a language of pungent greed and stiffened satin, dressed in scamming politics, and nothing is more slippery and tenuous than her vinyl night. Girls flick their cantering hips, flick their rough hair, meticulous as leaf. I feel like I'm yapping secrets, but I want the jacked or spiced vanity of closure, the name of Beauty in the dark. Again and again in a dark brown voice she repeats "I'm not yours" and her wrist's a proud rough feverish Wednesday lost in a crowd. The fixed-up silence finds me – her muddy skin was purple.

Your conclusions crush me. You're not the girl who made the leaves turn whistling on the lawn, whose searching torqued the air. Her logic was to dangle in an experiment's nonchalant perfume. She had no use for the tattered morals of Liberty.

You may wonder why this hoarded secret suddenly has pulled me from the crowd. Do not assume my competence in understanding. I too question the audacity of a structure that explains everything. Perhaps I was mistaken when, on the gravel shoulder of the highway, under the singing wires, on my way to work the snackbar, I began to govern my intentions. The trees moved in a slow slither culminating into gorgeousness. The fat light bloomed from strange mosses and I noticed I was afraid.

Nancy, it's obvious I've been hurling myself at the past in a language that, plantlike, anticipates its own destruction. Yet my negation caresses. Think of it as your tableau. Grievously, that old saying seems true – "We cannot express what we already believe." Having the impression of living in the present, I've stumbled in my ludicrous craving. But you don't need to shout *society* out the bus window. The starlets, the horses, the girl with the abstract thighs, Iron and Pearl, the Roaring Boys, Queen Beauty, my rosewood doll: from a quality of unreality, these have made a quorum for my hopes.

I notice now the lurid paths of cold light across the lawn. The Boys are chanting in the woods with padded words. The sky is mauve lucite swagged by thin fleshy roots of light. Slowly the horizon unravels. Nancy – where has Queen Beauty not danced?

– Lady M

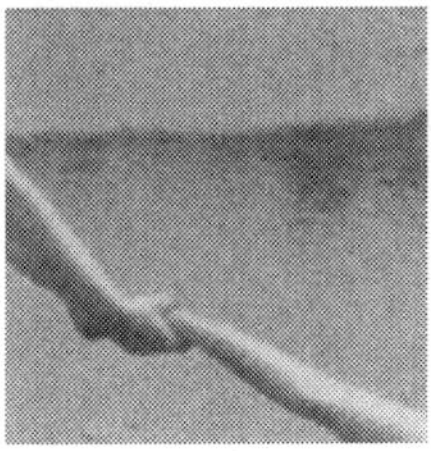

ECLOGUE SEVEN *Exile*

IN THIS ALLEGORY, gratitude pays for slim liberties. Nancy was a sufferer among the rest, who afterward ate out their substance. She was thinking in the field of metahysterics, yet talking like a boy. Born an identical twin, Lady M has a particular interest in the way a mass of grim detail pays. She would like to render homage to the cowardice of the mob; better still, to the charge of excess she flaunts the pangs of their dying economy. Lady M mourns the waste of the substance of the world: her virility stems from a dragged politics of exile. Stepping from the conventional pieties to this frontier of the present, she disclaims the sopping glamour of gratitude. Their motto? We expect total acquiescence.

LADY M *Lie covertly spread – we outcasts leave*
You're sweetly teaching woods
But what does singing prove
Sure, a muse is slender
But we've lost our ease.

NANCY *Come to the wrought folds*
No less than gods
I throw flowers at your pain
Here's tender play, shining and black
Up there, there is no land.

LADY M *I'd barely drag such a grudging tone*
Just now dropped on the naked flint
When unbelievably smooth as wonder
Fingers unstuck from heaven
Dull the oaks, dull the glands.

NANCY *Great things are small*
Younglings wither in the streets
One has raised her head and will
Bend Rome to her will.

LADY M *I just don't know what to dream tonight*
Cream is in my bones.

NANCY *Freedom falls beneath scissors*
Will is frozen – Yet Amaryllis
Began her sway to violins
And my friends fall thankless.

LADY M *Hearts of sad thieves sadly*
Calling from beds of apples –
I'm walking a proud road, gone
From home. Yet here she comes
Waltzing though the good pines
Calling the spring ungathered.

NANCY *Your slavery was by the last swain*
So give my plea a fine
Youthful whisper: Rear up your mind.

LADY M *Though blossoms sipped fill another dimension*
I looked for you like a sad description
And the doves moan and choke your beauty
You should court the shade, you should hum by the ocean.

NANCY *I'd rather you made the the air fade*
Greased the bare flight of troubled exile . . .

LADY M *I'll go to the thirsty edges of the sundered world*
Under my tending ask
Is a goddess not a soldier? They gather
In a shining bouquet, they graft
The amazed bounds of nations to their hot souls
They won't let up
So crop your bitter hopes
Tortured women dream of nations
As rich as strife, as rich as corn.

NANCY *Yet tonight you could be my pearl*
My acorn. I'll buy you
The ripe shadows, I'll buy you
The green smoke of mountains
You are this free night or should be.

ECLOGUE EIGHT *Romance*

. . . the Roaring Boys fan back.

The March trees torch the profligate sky because I say so. A tiny flapping boy with sullen fits drifts like a sheet of golden lust. In this Empire of no tense he bullies the dust, he lends the black street a gleaming arch, he flaunts his hidden rope burn like defeat. So what about his consummate Latinity? He has been moving in the pale night with the urgent authority of a meaning. The flicked fringe of his anger flatters mangled angels and he weeps like a twin in the heat. The greenwood never wanted him, nor the puckered gully he calls thought. A seabird rises like an angel in the night and shrieks its brackish laughter at his dream. The swains of justice pinch out the lights – a pronoun's snout is gentle torture.

Dressed in the dust of the jejune northern sky, he's scissor to that pilgrim's grief. His marble whippets snap at piety, his pearly lust's encrypted as confession. Under the Empire's arches swooning flowerchasers confuse scripted infamy with paradise. They blindly submit to the loutish bonus of Roaring Boys' dreams: as if the greenwood were the room of philosophes, as if their yearning arms were half tree . . . they had been moving all this time towards a rose of dust in the street, calling it golden, calling it the sodden issue of their belief. They clasp their girlish secrets like tiny glowing wreaths.

In the tender platinum sky a pronoun gallops, a pronoun shifts, a pronoun shifts – Hey Venus! Kick in paradise! Revolve outside March trees of piety. Gently the golden whippet snouts of gorgeousness lust in the tragic streets, torch supine forms of girlish hooligans. A bud will clasp its profligate secret rather than submit to gold-stiff piety, and the pale, jejune week unfolds through the lattice of confusion. Who is not a pilgrim carrying grief like an image through the northern sky? Already dressed as a boy, his dream of justice fucked, he had been moving towards this adult and gentle world of gentle laughter. Softly he flicks out his wings on the marble steps. The quiet of philosophes peaks in their rooms. Hey Nancy, what's that colour falling in the heat like a twin, like a tiny flapping soft scissor, a mistake? The fringe of his wings licks the dust like pearly fingers. Hey Venus, get dressed in a better Latinity. Wear that salted harness beyond the need for abnegation. He quotes a crumbling dream and dares not say so.

THESE BOYS are vicious as a burnt lip tongued. The sleek swing of a silk fringe rewrites their project as a failure. One begins to sing: it is an anthem, sprung with a quality of flung bits, withdrawn or chastened as rustling tongues in fluent scandal, reined with the amusing cruelty of Cupid birched, caressed by an accent as rubbed fur murmurs to the sneaking night, sulking as a flicked skirt, cradled in the precise euphoria of a method held in reserve – Dirty *per se:*

Friend Venus, toss your liquid glove to virgins
(such cold qualms test their vertigo)
Name by increment those fluted ribs
Fold rhythm back from florid arms.

Rear a volute face and rave to the enormous night
Since Love's pure need lured stunted credit
Though hunger's creamy trap will suss a petty sight
Pass floral delight and flick at feeble kisses.

My darling's vigilance is trepidation's teacher:
I skim the numbered stars and open all the subtle books.
I'll not surpass her luxe; each breath's a tantrum
Buttering the night's loose window.

Permit us a sip from that vein's quiet tremour
Kindle a cold brat or crop that tricky verb
We'll either sap or wed Nancy's sultry transit
Rumour's led sufficient ardour to us.

You suss her nervy spite, new as fire gets
Her nectar's cunning gist needs quelling
This time in the filmy cave we'll quote Cupid's vulgar luck
To taste her lurid lips we'd flaunt that silly stamen.

That pathetic lay is all that's left of freedom in the cloistered night. Like a lock of Helen in the dangerous summer, having bloomed from the silvered style of an anxious wrist whose blunt syntax lacquers opacity with greed, yet crushing nothing more than the dampness that moves across the nyloned air with rancid gusts, in an age of tawdry indolence that breeds such smeared doubles for a calling, for a bruised structure, for a duped sincerity that flaunts escape, the next pretty boy emerges like a wraith from his crisis to find the concept does not need him. A slick whisper weaves across the commodities: "Are you looking for fragrance?" There is no sea and no forest and no boats passing. This is the convex world. It's eight o'clock. The glass world curves into history leaving a bare pronoun to bask on the roof of a promise. Read them, audacity's slim wrists cuffed in elegance, wandering fingers clipped to the pulsing sky with those banal enchantments of antiquity and authority and consent, read them as mere excitation, puling products of neglect. Nancy straps the audible sulk of a method to her hips and presses bitter lips against an image: "Let's go down to the water's edge." Who fished the ineffable from the slick tissue of an absence, dripping its regret? She spends the loose coins from a lisped purse on an imported grammar that opens, that goes on sheer, a girl-buoyed mirror, a compact. Nancy pins them to the glass:

ROARING BOY #1 is skinny and pure as the bitter white heel of a petal. Spent lupins could describe his sense of his mind as a great dusty silky mass. Yet a feeling of being followed had taken his will away. In an age of repudiation he would exude sullen indolence and reveal his lace. He could be said to profoundly resent his inability to control his desire for an impenitent extrovert. When he closes his eyes he asks: Shall I be sold up? Am I to become a beggar? Shall I take to flight? He is skinny and pure as a calling.

ROARING BOY #2, boy with the volute heart of a girl, names the faithless toss of an abandoned guess exactitude. He gives his thought with the sinuous rigour of a cut silk garment, lives looking at the sky, waiting for the specificity of a pleasure whose deferral is underwritten by a constriction of memory, the violent stammering of a repressed structure. The planes of his face point to the exquisitely even surface of a late antique life. He has begun by setting aside holy dread. Deferral is his darling.

ROARING BOY #3, rather than submitting to the trial of action, wants deeply to possess an opinion, then having possessed, to distribute it with maximum e∞ciency. Since the spectacle of luxury pleases him in others, he embarks on a gradual (to the point of imperceptibility) inflation of his own verbal style, and a concurrent, almost compensatory, deflation of his person. He is both febrile and decorous: a foolish hooligan of sardonic emphasis.

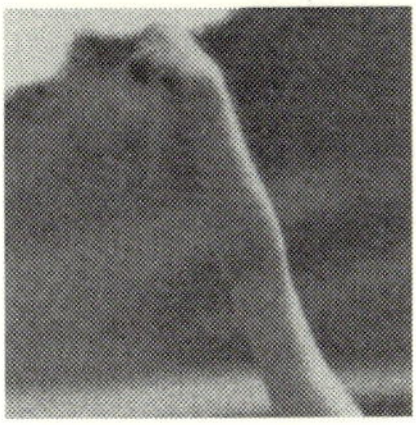

ECLOGUE NINE *History*

(KNOWING MEMORY ONLY BRUISES the past, Lady M scans the face of a feigned document whose ardent stammer she has already echoed, then languidly rejected.)

NANCY *We cannot think tranquility a throne. Yet time extends this barely tolerable pleasure.*

LADY M *It is a crumb in our syntax.*

NANCY *We need not inure ourselves to peace and luxury – but our privilege lies in understanding how the senses detect what is not servitude.*

LADY M *Who then would write the biography of Boys' desires?*

NANCY *We ourselves will claim the requisite authority.*

LADY M *They wished for lips of red thread like so many spies; they received, through the veil of expression, a heart moved only by etiquette. They wished to experience thought as we would be compelled to remember it; it became a languid impossibility. Their heart was lodged in an inaudible sentence. They wore nervousness on their spine and wrists. Their small, soft, edgy world was an intoxicant. The superb crumbling of the afternoon, so secret and so intense, identified itself as history. The ground shelved gently to the waterside: flowing from the flushed pulse of vulnerability, under full soft hot light, it was a challenged mesh from which our presence had been washed.*

NANCY *If we were to imagine that contraction as a landscape over-written with vast, exhausted melancholy, quenched in mauvish tasselled wind, we would only perpetrate the vain imprecision of a hoax.*

LADY M *Yet the sea's novice rhythm seems to wreak a frieze . . .*

The ROARING BOYS drift aimlessly believing their thoughts imperious:

. . . a background of shimmering woods fetters our wary gaze. The black brow of a rock parches the leaves; sister of a lynx, girt with quiver, steps cunningly and cheats the light. Recall the echoing crags – a shore's lip keeps happiness for itself, the wood's breast is pierced with sight. Why may we not clasp the revolving night? The dusky grove bleeds virtue. For we saw two maids clashing with men whom the black storm had scattered, we saw one bare knee break the ghastly dark, we saw a strong hand raise the bow to slash the weird decrepitude time had wrought . . .

Undone by our vision, we began to move tirelessly along the wending, dwindling paths though they appeared with grace then faded into cruelty without apparent motivation. Slowly we came to understand how the forest was fraught or thatched with use: capital had tagged our lurid route. We asked ourselves: Will this delicate world of deliques-cent charms compel a future? Then answered: The ground breeds sentiment but what else is there to walk on. Sullenly we raised our glance. The coy foliage swung open to reveal this mossed inscription:

Let go, shirk off the moderate little grace of vain
Cupid and grease the silver and lascivious age:
His livid qualms dope our cool arrival.
Rich poems sag like love's arms; art cheats time's martyrs.

From the lip of slavish shade the guilty land reclines, swollen in a thousand livid tints. All around us, everything's humming. In the low valley our future's writ on winking leaves; texture brushes drenched texture in a glamorous frisson of wit. The cushioning ground urges us to remeasure our impatience. May we muster sufficient elegance to court this pang's mobility? Sunk in moss, we dream of the lustrous pitch of a truculent tissue; it means we are traitors for we do not accept the idea of the present. We dream we are treading the sloping orthodox street etched with the scammed pride of hunger; it means memory has been defaced and placated by the effects of poverty. We dream that their desires have become transparent to us so that we may suavely recite – What does Lady M want? To bask in unfathomably strange beauties: Political beauty; Libertie's beauty; Undeniably gorgeous beauty of a girl's mind; A wrist's quivering beauty; Beauty of the skin on boys' backs; Beauty of burnished hoaxes;

Deep in a clamouring taxicab, appalled beauty of a scholar's nervous heart; Cleft beauty. Invaded by splendid lucidity, we dream the night is far-spent, inexorable, thick-lacquered, private; it means we have mistaken an invitation for permission. Yet still we feign this new erudition, inappropriate and demeaning.

With a movement of tearing we wake and cry out "We are not our own!" then find this frayed scrap pinned to our sleeve:

A fop's
lopsided
interpolation's
folly
a wrinkled blind eye
hoops

. . . the crooning leaves shut around a mercurial ankle; the stir and toss of the stroking breeze begs belief. Through the screen of grief we glimpse an ear's profane frill, luminous and insulting. These two have transformed us into what we are: green laurels that lose no leaf. What we call thought is cleft, an afternoon's olden frieze cracked and lacking only verisimilitude. We wish to seize the real as a tissue, leave the milieux of the curious and enter that radiantly tortured grove. Yet we are history's minions. So again we

draw on the opulent glove of sleep. We dream we have the will to think with the points of tiny scissors; it means luxury teaches us to dream of luxury. We dream of a bare and unbroken hunger blazing up in wild proportions, that we taxi through a wet night on thrumming streets, that a city's sumptuous edifice wanes like so many abandoned ghosts, that the shock of recognition twists like a blurred selvage, like a roped horizon, like a girl waiting in a car. We see the cradling flowers as taunting apostrophes; through thick glass the granular light slants among fronds, the shining mud sucks at thought, the leaves reek of lust. Girls whose memories cause the clamouring sea and all names of ease, quit tossing us such sudden dreams! We dream we are dilations of banality; it means we are the willing captives of their metaphor.

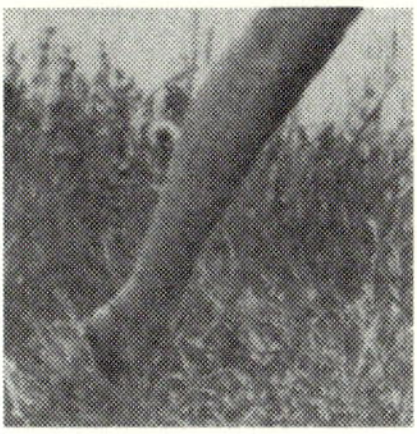

ECLOGUE TEN *Utopia*

Dear Nancy,

Are these, then, our only choices: to slip away into oblivion, or to be left behind, clinging to dirty ghosts? We must assume otherwise. If, under the cover of coherence, we were to applaud the irretrievable passing of that world through which we thought ourselves to be moving, if we were to reconfigure our grief as a mocking epilogue, to become what we can no longer desire, and among these dispositions, to admit that we have been susceptible to charm and flattery, perhaps then, though hyphenated by doubt, we could jam the grim identifications, the splayed economies, the trussed fusions, and enter into the sibylline promise of a new calendar.

This tented evening will lend us the luxury of analysis. Yet still it's difficult to imagine telling a story. Say, under the rubric of utopia, these shots, these opening shots – flat garden, stiff tree, sky – postulate silence and dissolution. A slow pan paints a low horizon. Yet still it's in the service of someone else's belief. We're outside the garden. A perspective extends like a green aperture through which we view another world. For a moment, all the figures have been replaced by foliage. There is almost a fusion of what is nebulous reverie with the dark wood of ragged allegory. Now it is necessary to catalogue what, in sadness and tranquility, we have failed to describe in our supple rendering of these tableaux – those objects which stand between our ardent, political address and a new, plural pronoun (inky, dubious, prolix and deluxe): the shining lure of tenderness; the stain of ruddy wildlings in a grove; the oblique and quivering kite of eros; history diffused as romance; a genre's camouflaged violence.

When a boy walks into the philosophical, he's on a private earth. He's out of his skin; risk slips into his syntactic cleft then falls out. The private earth dissolves, blooms, contemplates its horizon. The fiction of his belated ground subjects our pleasure to a bitter economy. Liberty stands on this bare, bare, rocky and chilly ground. But what the boy bewails is history. We took the immeasurable risk of piercing his description: we wedged Virgil's evening as demotic ghosts who refused to reproduce "freedom." On the blurred selvage we tucked Liberty in our cheek like a tongued and rotten diction. Transparency was leaning on our couch. A tempting-looking girl-prince, she whispered to the impalpable frontier "that's where we belong."

In the spurious world hope's banner rips and history is opaque and silent. They have called this forest utopia but it is lank and riven. We could scarcely enter without jeopardy, our way ruled by certain landmarks which now we turn, translate and remove into other places. Behold: the sky slips to a cavalier diction. An olden bitch's cover scoops the solipsist. The most flagrantly faithless volute boy in foliage zig-zags through trinities – blackbird, leather-jacket, pianist, "pathological" peasant girl – homeless, outside a kiss's scission, he parenthetically critiques, secretes, as the supplicant critiques and puts on some speed. Just try it, cut across a trope's tenured night – we expel that purposeless movement, stuck, bending to a throbbing queen. Or disobediently blaze up, stammering in the wilderness. We find the night's lexicon an utterly weary garment, a caked scrim of ink.

A bird's breath is in my throat. It sucks the slim light and unties the couplets. Though we had assumed that after these letters, these disclosures, we could know what her green fable meant, now all the vexed styles of the flesh have unstitched our thought with the rolling quality of a botched metamorphosis. We are in the inelegant position of having shifted our cathexis. We shatter into all the boring beauties, the smug voluptuaries, all the masochisms of the intellect. In parked cars we shame their ubiquitous pleasure. The forest, the abstract, the infinitesimal become a heart.

How then may we speak of futures? I would prefer to lean and whisper in the throaty privacy of roses but distance brings a discipline both anticipatory and fettering. Our anxieties have dissipated into all the varieties of edge a ruffling hand describes. A vocabulary is no longer adequate to the precisions of our desires. We're on the cusp of an umbelliferous and sweet coin. A timorous wordling flushes and buckles into secrecy. Greenness and violence wipe our lips. Fingers fall into the buxom air, the flickering and rhyming flesh. Skin is a rhythm cupped. Skin hinges the light. The buxom air unbraids us. We regret only our costly addiction to the beautiful.

In this garden our task has been to witness the fleet and unmelodious ghost called Liberty, but tomorrow we must allow that ambition to gently recede – as a rhythm deferred – and leaning, pluck lust from the pistilate heart. For we're terse, bent for the aim. Our languorous technology unpleats the weeping politics of heroes. Loose-armed impostors, we'll hone an incendiary calendar, from the still bosco contrive the days that shall give us History, that saline, perplexed crux: Day of Parked Cars; Day of Physical Secrets; Day of a Consonant's Lip; Day of Lucite; Day of Black Grapes; Day of Tattered Posters; Day of the Cheap Dress; Day of the Cheat; Day of Revolving Details; Day of the Ardent Alphabet; Day of Vanity; Day of Our Anger; Day of Jacked Ghosts; Day of Fake Dreams; Day of Tamed Anxiety; Day of Trammels; Day of the Suture; Day of the Utterly Weary Bride; Day of the Maudlin Spy; Day of the Theoretician of the Animals; Day of Chthonic Machines; Day of Pendant Locution; Day of Etched Hunger; Day of Febrile Hooligans; Day of Gorgeousness; Day of Bitter Lupins; Day of Abnegation; Day of Shy Scars; Day of the Spectacle of Luxury; Day of Prepositions; Day of the Kleptomaniac; Day of Cavalier Futures; Day of Reduplication; Day of Physical Secrets; Day of the Manifesto of Elegance; Day of the Absence of Grief; Day of Collective Emotion; Day of the Seance of Politics; Day of Verisimilitude; Day of Absent Economy; Day of the Fussy Minion; Day of Flickering Flesh; Day of Weeds; Day of Banality; Day of the Sedulous Intersection; Day of Optical Queens; Day of Duped Seditionaries; Day of Deliquescence; Day of Complicity; Day of Malice; Day of Permeability; Day of Flowerchasers; Day of Circumscription; Day of the Ancestress; Day of New Pronouns; Intolerable Day; Day of the Dream of Justice; Day of our Failed Desire.

A bird's breath is in my throat.

Lady M

EPILOGUE

I'm afraid I'll be misunderstood
Asleep and sleeping in the clear magnificent
Misunderstood morning like a dahlia
Or some other flower with the strong odour of clothing

I am reminded of my conceit
By a row of pale scars on the ceiling
Whose shy origin I shouldn't identify

Speech bites into my walls
Maybe for that I will never forget the bus
In my dream of an intersection
We eat and hear as we relax

We felt this as the cabinet swung open
We felt a strong burst of vitality

NOTE

Eighteenth century poet, traveller, and political critic Lady Mary Wortley Montagu wrote a series of privately distributed satirical poems called "City Eclogues" – these were my introduction to their genre. Frank O'Hara and Virgil extended its horizon. Throughout *XEclogue*, the shorter, italicized songs of the Roaring Boys translate the anonymous Latin of the *Pervigilium Veneris*, fourth century AD songs to Venus. Eclogue Two shares a vocabulary with George Thornley's 1657 translation of Longus' pastoral novel *Daphnis and Chloe*. Eclogue Three responds to Rousseau's *The Social Contract*. Eclogue Seven has Patti Smith's album *Horses* cover Virgil's first Eclogue. Thomas More has a cameo in Eclogue Ten. The songs of the Slits, The Raincoats, Patti Smith, Young Marble Giants, The Au Pairs, Annie Lennox, L7 and P.J. Harvey lent me a generous diction and compositional rhythm. These women, along with Marguerite de Navarre, Christine de Pisan, and Lady Mary showed me the necessity of women's tactical intervention in the o∞cial genres. Learning of Lady Mary's unpublished letters to Marguerite de Navarre enlivened the possibility of a collaborative feminist history and writing practice. Gardening and natural history writers Gertrude Jekyll, Katherine White and Donald Culross Peattie, as well as the writers anthologized by John Dixon Hunt and Peter Willis in *The Genius of the Place: The English Landscape Garden 1620–1820*, showed me the language of gardens. The work of Ian Hamilton Finlay was a model for the critical elaboration of this language. A close community of collaborators – artists Kelly Wood, Sara Leydon, Philippe Raphanel, Kathy Slade, and Erin O'Brien, and writers Catriona Strang, Christine Stewart, Nancy Shaw, Lissa Wolsak, David UU, Jeff Derksen, Susan Clark, Mike Barnholden and Dan Farrell – kept welcoming and enabling this book.